Sebastian Sigloch

How does Open Innovation in Information Technology affect the

An inevitable snowball - effect

I0012871

GRIN - Verlag für akademische Texte

Der GRIN Verlag mit Sitz in München hat sich seit der Gründung im Jahr 1998 auf die Veröffentlichung akademischer Texte spezialisiert.

Die Verlagswebseite www.grin.com ist für Studenten, Hochschullehrer und andere Akademiker die ideale Plattform, ihre Fachtexte, Studienarbeiten, Abschlussarbeiten oder Dissertationen einem breiten Publikum zu präsentieren.

Document Nr. V184981

Sebastian Sigloch

How does Open Innovation in Information Technology affect the Business Development

An inevitable snowball - effect

GRIN Verlag

Bibliografische Information der Deutschen Nationalbibliothek: Die Deutsche Bibliothek verzeichnet diese Publikation in der Deutschen Nationalbibliografie; detaillierte bibliografische Daten sind im Internet über http://dnb.d-nb.de/ abrufbar.

Dieses Werk sowie alle darin enthaltenen einzelnen Beiträge und Abbildungen sind urheberrechtlich geschützt. Jede Verwertung, die nicht ausdrücklich vom Urheberrechtsschutz zugelassen ist, bedarf der vorherigen Zustimmung des Verlages. Das gilt insbesondere für Vervielfältigungen, Bearbeitungen, Übersetzungen, Mikroverfilmungen, Auswertungen durch Datenbanken und für die Einspeicherung und Verarbeitung in elektronische Systeme. Alle Rechte, auch die des auszugsweisen Nachdrucks, der fotomechanischen Wiedergabe (einschließlich Mikrokopie) sowie der Auswertung durch Datenbanken oder ähnliche Einrichtungen, vorbehalten.

1. Auflage 2011
Copyright © 2011 GRIN Verlag GmbH
http://www.grin.com
Druck und Bindung: Books on Demand GmbH, Norderstedt Germany
ISBN 978-3-656-13201-1

How does Open Innovation in Information Technology
affect the Business Development as an inevitable
snowball - effect

Bachelor-Thesis

Fakultät Informatik
Hochschule Reutlingen
Reutlingen University
Studiengang Wirtschaftsinformatik

Bearbeiter
Sebastian Sigloch

28.06.2011

Table of Contents

German abstract

Die Öffnung des Innovationsprozesses von Organisationen ist in der heutigen Forschung & Entwicklung ein wichtiger Schritt, um sich der Ideen und des Wissens der Außenwelt als strategisches Werkzeug zu Nutze zu machen. Jedoch gibt es keinerlei Artikel, welche Auswirkungen die Implementierung von "Offenen Innovationen" in der Unternehmensentwicklung haben. Diese Bachelorthesis soll hierfür den Nutzen von "Offenen Innovationen" im IT - Service Bereich, sowohl in der Forschung & Entwicklung als auch deren Übertragung in die strategische Unternehmensentwicklung aufzeigen und mögliche Schneeballeffekte definieren. Die Untersuchungen zeigten, dass die Implementierung von "Offenen Innovationen" in das Unternehmen einen maßgeblichen Einfluss auf die Unternehmensentwicklung und die Wettbewerbsfähigkeit hat. Durch diese Bachelorthesis erlangt der Leser einen Überblick über die Beziehung zwischen "Offenen Innovationen" und deren strategischen Nutzen.

Besonderer Dank geht an meine beiden Betreuer, Herrn Prof. Dr. rer. pol. Gerhard Killy von der Hochschule Reutlingen und Herrn Dr. Rob Dekkers von der UWS Business School, University of the West of Scotland, die es mir ermöglicht haben, meine Bachelorthesis über dieses Thema anzufertigen. Ich danke Ihnen für die vielseitige Unterstützung und Betreuung meiner Bachelorthesis. Desweiteren möchte ich allen Personen danken, die mich bei meiner Bachelorthesis und bei meinem Studium unterstützt und begleitet haben.

English abstract

The opening - up of the innovation processes within organizations is an important step in today's Research & Development in order to take advantage from both, external knowledge and ideas as strategic instruments. However there are no articles about the influences for implementation of Open Innovations into the Business Development. Therefore this dissertation should demonstrate the utilization of Open Innovations within the IT - Service field for both, the Research & Development and their assignment within the Business Development. Furthermore possible snowball - effects should be defined as well. The investigations showed up, that the implementation of Open Innovations have a major impact on the Business Development as well as the competitive advantage of an organization. With this dissertation the reader obtain an overview over the relationship between Open Innovations and their strategically usage.

Special thanks are going to both of my advisors, Prof. Dr. rer. pol. Gerhard Killy from the Reutlingen University and to Dr. Rob Dekkers from the UWS Business School, University of the West of Scotland, which made it possible to write my dissertation about this topic. Thanks to all persons, which supported and accompanied me during my dissertation and my whole studies.

Purpose of this thesis / dissertation

The main purpose of this document is, to answer the following thesis / dissertation question:

> How does Open Innovation in IT affect the Business Development as an inevitable snowball effect?

However problem -or question solving implicates a fragmentation of the defined problem or question into subproblems or subquestions. Therefore the following questions have been determined beforehand and should be answered at the end of this thesis / dissertation as well as explained with a string of examples:

1. What is Open Innovation ? - differentiation and integration
2. How is the Open Innovation - paradigm used within IT - Services?
3. Is there a relationship between the implementation of Open Innovation and the Business Development?
4. Is it possible, that the implementation of the Open Innovation - paradigm leads to competitive advantage?
5. Can the mutation from the Closed Innovation - paradigm to the Open Innovation - paradigm lead to an inevitable snowball effect?

The document overview can be illustrated by the following process, where the questions 1 - 5 can be again recognized as well.

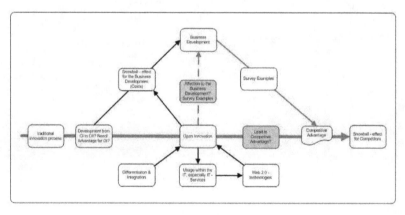

Process Overview 1

In order to analyze the above mentioned thesis as well as the subproblems or subquestions, the following methods will be used iteratively:

- wide literature research within the fields Open Innovation, Information Technology as well as Business Development
- evaluation if the determined issues have been achieved
- detailed literature research within the fields Open Innovation and Information Technology
- evaluation if the determined issues have been achieved
- possible revision of a literature research
- sighting of the information, determining of relationships within the information
- building a concept on basis of the information which had been found
- evaluation of the concept and verbal check
- de novo evaluation to the issues
- possible adaptation of the final version regarding the issues

List of abbreviations

FLL	First Lego League
IP	Intellectual Property
IPO	Initial Public Offering
ITRI	Industrial Technology Research Institute
MITS	Micro Instrumentation and Telemetry Systems
OECD	Organisation for Economic Co-Operation and Development
OIC	Open Innovation Center
PARC	Palo Alto Research Center, Xerox

1   The Open Innovation - paradigm

Within the first chapter, the Open Innovation - paradigm should be differentiated from the traditional, Closed Innovation - paradigm. In order to illustrate changes in Research & Development, an historical approach will show up the differences between the ways of innovating. Furthermore the Open Innovation approach will be integrated and evaluated traditionally. Additionally this chapter should show up possible implementations of the Open Innovation - paradigm within the IT Service industry, especially the usage of Web 2.0 technologies, by using a string of examples.

1.1   Early innovating and Research & Development changes

In the early days', the Research & Development was seen as the treasure of an organization. D. Nobelius [Nobe04] showed up 5 generations of Research & Development management (cf. Table 1). Early Adopters like the Marshall Space Flight Center [Msfc11] in Alabama acquired external knowledge in the 1950's in order to develop their rockets technology, which were necessary for their Apollo 11 mission, which had the target to land on the moon.[1],[2],[3] Hence spaceflight technologies as well as electronics, computers and radio technologies became part of the 20th century innovations.[4] Research & Development management became, regarding to D. Nobelius [Nobe04] part of the corporate strategies and were integrated moving-away from a product focus, towards a customer integration. Nowadays the information technology industry as well as the economically benefits of innovation and education became important parts of the upcoming changes during the 21st century.[5] The processes of innovation, which should help companies utilizing and advancing technologies in order to create new products and services, were explained by Chesbrough [Ches06] as "A Tale of Two Models", which will be closer looked at in chapter 1.2.[6] For the 21st century success, the Open Innovation - paradigm · seems to be an important factor within the Research & Development. Innovation is expensive. Companies are finding it increasingly difficult to justify increasing R&D costs.[7] In regards to Henry Chesbrough [Chesb06]

---

[1] see also: [Nasa69]: Apollo 11 Technical Air-to-Ground Voice transcription
[2] see also: [Ross06]: Important Events in Human History
[3] see also: [Hahn07]: Wernher von Braun - Vater aller Raketen
[4] see also: [Coso03]: A Century of Innovation: Twenty Engineering Achievements that Transformed our Lives, p. 7 et seq.
[5] see also: [Naas97]: Preparing for the 21st century - Technology and the nation's future
[6] see also: [Ches06]: Open Innovation - The New Imperative for Creating and Profiting from Technology, p. 17
[7] see also: [Chesb06]: Open Business Models: How to Thrive in the New Innovation Landscape

this is enhanced by decreasing product revenues due to shorter product life cycles for example within the Electronic or IT sectors. Additionally companies require greater knowledge, regarding to Bowonda et al. [Bowo05] in order to compete more markets within the globalizing world. In regards to Fetterhoff & Voelkel [Fett06] the values of companies lies in their brands rather than in the ability to invent products or manufacture them. This implicates the "outsourcing" of innovation as well as divesting of productions.[8] In regards to Henry Chesbrough [Ches03], no single company knows everything. Additionally knowledge has become distributed in universities as well as in web-based communities (cf. Chapter 1.3.2) and we are witnessing the obsolescece of Research & Development in many industries. D. Nobelius [Nobe04] mentioned, that the new generation of Research & Development is taking place with cross-boundary alliances. These alliances involve company networks and the new generation of Research & Development is focusing on the integration of different systems. [9] Thus Open Innovation should provide new ways to create value outside the firm boundaries.

R&D generations	Process Characteristics
First generation	R&D as ivory tower
1950 to mid- 1960's	technology - push oriented
Second generation	R&D as business
Mid- 1960s to early 1970s	market - pull oriented
Third generation	R&D as portfolio
Mid- 1970s to mid-1980s	Linkage to corporate strategy
Fourth generation	R&D as integrative activity
Early 1980s to mid-1990s	Implementing of customers
Fifth generation	R&D as network
Mid-1990s onward	Involving external ideas & knowledge

Table 1: Altered Table: Description of five R&D generations, cf. [Nobe04]

---

[8] see also: [Fett06]: Managing Open Innovation in Biotechnology
[9] see also: [Nobe04]: Towards the sixth generation of R&D management, p.4

1.2   The opening up and mutation of the traditional - paradigm culminating in the Open Innovation - paradigm

Eva Galli [Gall08] mentioned, that researchers and managers in the field of technology "associated strong internal Research & Development capabilities with innovativeness".[10] Thus ideas and knowledge were generated within an organization's own Research & Development laboratories. Market diffusion was, regarding to Eva Galli [Gall08] distributed by their traditional distribution channels. This autonomous way of innovation management has been called Closed Innovation by Henry Chesbrough [Ches06] for which he traced the following six implicit principles:

- The smartest people in a companies industry should work for them
- To profit from Research & Development, we must discover, develop, produce and ship it ourselves
- If we discover it ourselves, we will get it to market first
- If we are the first to commercialize an innovation, we will win
- If we create the most and best ideas in the industry, we will win
- We should control our intellectual property (henceforth.: IP) so that our competitors do not profit from ideas

The logic of the CI paradigm created a doom loop (cf. Figure 1)

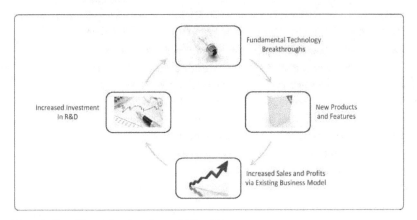

Figure 1: Closed Innovation doom loop, cf. [Ches06]

This doom loop show up, that increasing investments within the Research & Development will lead to fundamental technology breakthroughs. These breakthroughs lead to, like the before mentioned rules explained, to new

---

[10] see also: [Gall08]: Building Social Capital in a Multibusiness Firm, p.23

products and features. These new products will increase the sales and profits via the existing Business Model. The gained profit can be invested again into the Research & Development and let the doom loop restart again. Furthermore the intellectual property, which arise from the internal Research & Development is, like in the beforehand mentioned rules as well, closely guarded so that competitors don't get possibilities for profiting from other's Research & Development findings. The following graphic (cf. Figure 2) which has been modelled after Henry Chesbrough [Ches06] should explain the flow of ideas and Research Projects within the Research & Developement funnel.

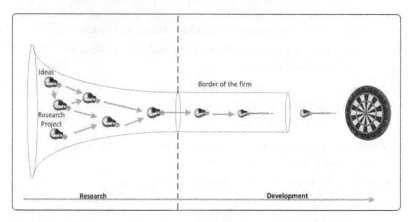

Figure 2: The Closed Innovation paradigm for Managing R&D, cf. [Reic06];[Ches06]

Ideas as well as Research Projects enter in the funnel at the left side of Figure 2. Subsequently these Research Projects's as well as the ideas from scientists or research employees within the Research & Development department will be proceeded and transformed within the boundaries of the organization. In doing so, the funnel is acting like a filter in order to get rid of false Research Projects and ideas. Finally the combination from Research Projects and ideas will be developed and later launched on the determined target market to reach the customer.

Alterations of the former abiotic environment led to jiggle the underpinnings of the Closed Innovation paradigm. According to Henry Chesbrough [Ches06] it seems obvious that since education factors, which include a burgeoning amount of university - trainings as well as postgraduate trainings, the knowledge is distributed and not concentrated to company-trainings anymore. Moreover these highly skilled and experienced people undergo a growing mobility. Thus concluded in highly capable start-up companies, which could use the growing presence of private venture capital in order to commercialize external research into valuable companies. Furthermore the increasingly fast time to market for products and services challenged the traditional approach of Figure 1. Customers gained knowledge from university graduates, what punched a hole in companies knowledge-edges. All these factors alter the approach of Closed Innovation and led according to Henry Chesbrough [Ches06] to a "new" approach, Open Innovation.

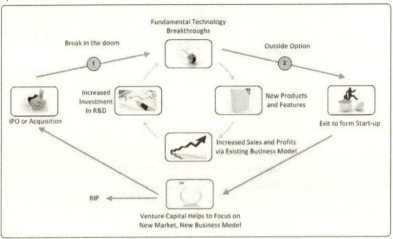

Figure 3: The broken doom loop

When a fundamental technology breakthrough due to increased Research & Development investment occured, then the researchers are aware of the possibility to leave the company in order to build a start up. (Point2 on Figure3). Like explained before the venture capital would help these start-up's to grow. Subsequently these start-ups either die, get an initial public offering or get acquired. For big companies these acquisitions are an easy way for entering in new markets as well as getting additionally knowledge of technologies, markets and their environment and management at an affordable price. However due to the initial public offering or acquisition of a start-up company there would occur a break in the doom loop (cf. Figure 1), which is visualized with Point 1 on Figure 3. Nevertheless it can be considered if these technology breakthroughs of outgoing researchers can be used in order to gain new breakthroughs in the Research & Development within the firm who acquires such start-up's. In regards to this proceedings the traditional Closed Innovation - paradigm, explained within Figure 2, can be extended by the following figure. Here occurs the need of the opening up of the firm boundaries in order to let more ideas as well as technologies flow into the own Research & Development funnel:[11]

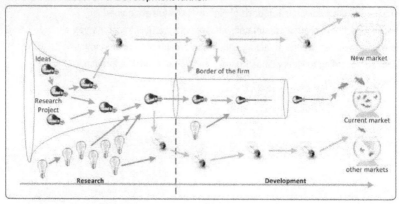

Figure 4: The Open Innovation paradigm for Managing R&D, cf. [Reic06];[Ches06]

The boundary of the firm is again displayed as a funnel in order to filter Research Project's. However the following extentions to the Closed Innovation - paradigm are clearly evidend as per arrow colour:

The figure above illustrates, that there are not just disadvantages with the mutation from the Closed Innovation - paradigm to the Open Innovation - paradigm. Like explained before the blue arrows show incoming Research Projects's, ideas or knowledge which could be used in order to get potential new technology breakthroughs. The green and the orange arrows from Figure4 showed the process of scientists who could leave the company with the knowledge or idea in their backpack. However these new processes and

---

[11] see also: [Ches06]: Open Innovation - The New Impertative for Creating and Profiting from Technology, p. 22 et seq.

ways to new or other markets, showed in B and C, can be used in order to eradicate former false Research Projects's. Serhan Ili [Sili09] stated, that due to a pointedly usage of external ideas as well as technologies, an organization is able to expand their actual innovation basis for their business activity.

The Design Against Crime Research Centre [Dacr11] extended the model of Figure4 by showing a possible inter-divisional approach of Open Innovation (Figure6). Each color would show another division of the company.

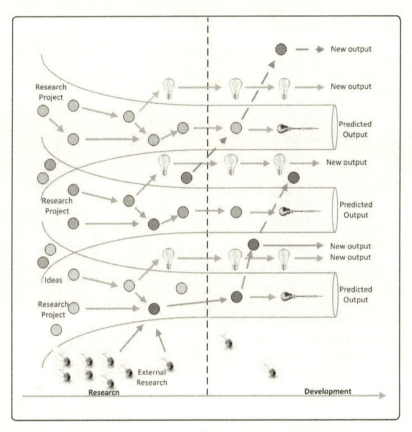

Figure 5: The OI - paradigm inter-divisional, cf. [Dacr11] ; [Reic06] ; [Ches06]

What this multi-disciplinary model of the Open Innovation - paradigm makes something special is, that Research Projects of different divisions move through the divisional boundaries. These boundaries are again porous in order to let ideas as well as Research Projects enter in and through. External Research Projects can enter the funnel as well. This coherences can lead to new outputs, what means new opportunities and improves our understanding of the possibilities within Open Innovation.[12] Moreover the multi-disciplinary Research & Development implicates new opportunities, which are showed in Figure7. These opportunities can be point out as well. The new outputs can induce hereby to three different opportunities:

- entering new markets
- entering other markets
- entering the current market

The normal Research & Development outputs induce hereby still the current market. This model show us, that Open Innovation helps to gain possibilities to expand the customer reach.

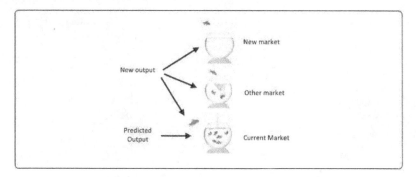

Figure 6: New Opportunities due to the multi-disciplinary model of [Dacr11]

Hence there's occurring knowledge which is carried out by scientists or employees in order to build a start-up (cf. Figure 4) the boundaries of the company or organization gets porous. Serhan Ili [Sili09] mentioned, that the Open Innovation - paradigm is an extension of the former business model. Henry Chesbrough [Ches06] stated, that a business model is "...a useful framework to link ideas and technologies to economic outcomes." Concluding the following three opportunities arise while using this new paradigm:

---

[12] see also: [Dacr11]: Why Open Innovation

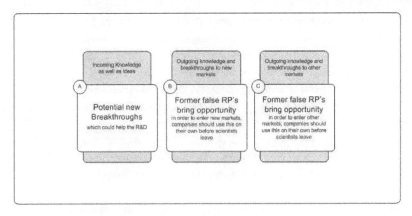

Figure 7: New Opportunities through the OI - paradigm

Henry Chesbrough [Ches06] stated that the mutation from the CI - paradigm to the OI - paradigm change the before mentioned implicit rules / principles:

Closed Innovation Principles	Open Innovation Principles
The smart people in out field work for us	Not all the smart people work for us. We need to work with smart people inside and outside our company
To profit from R&D, we must discover it, develop it, and ship it ourselves	External R&D can create significant value; internal R&D is needed to claim some portion of that value
If we discover it ourselves, we will get it to the market first	We don't have to originate the research to profit from it
The company that gets an innovation to market first will win	Building a better business model is better than getting to market first
If we create the most and the best ideas in the industry, we will win	If we make the best use of internal and external ideas, we will win
We should control our IP, so that our competitors don't profit from our ideas	We should profit from others' use of our IP, and we should buy others' IP whenever it advances our own business model.

Table 2: Contrasting Principles of the CI and the OI paradigm, cf. [Ches06], p. 26

However the idea to open up the Research & Development out of the firm boundaries is not a new train of thoughts. It seems that the Open Innovation - paradigm has its roots within the Stone Age. David Murray [Murr10] stated, that existing concepts have altered and combined to construct new concepts. A Neanderthal man could accidentially dislodged a large rock as he climed on a hill. The rock rolled down the slope and he thought about the first rock-wheel.[13] Thus implicates, that observations of the nature has been used as a kind of external information in order to develop something new. The first openness is born. External ideas have been borrowed and used for the own Research & Development. At a later time, these borrowing of ideas seemed to still apply. David Murray [Murr10] stated, that even Einstein's complex ideas were borrowed out of existing ideas. Even Einstein itself said: "The secret to creativity is knowing how to hide your sources".[14] In regards to David Murray [Murr10] Teresa Amabile from the Harvard Business School said, that "All innovation begins with creative ideas". Nowadays the open up of the Research & Development has been explored in Business since more than 50 years on how the best way to exploit knowledge from beyond the firm.[15] Trott & Hartmann [Trot09] determined the in Table 1 mentioned principles for the Closed Innovation as well as the Open Innovation - paradigm. Early adopter like Roy Allan [Alle69] and M. L. Tushman [Tush77] identified. Furthermore they explored that much technology and expertise is lying beyond the firm boundaries as well as who is collecting and exchanging knowledge and information on behalf of the firm. Thus findings are finally against the first principle of the Closed Innovation - paradigm, see also Table 1. Furthermore Trott & Hartmann [Trot09] determined, that since the 1970s many technology partnerships as well as new joint ventures between organizations arose rapidly. Thus implicated a fall of the going alone strategy. Businesses slowly broaden their view and formed strategic alliances. These alliances can be interpreted as a slowly opening up of the firms boundaries within their R&D processes. These changes refute the second Closed Innovation - paradigm principle. For the third principle there are some contradictions as well. Trott & Hartmann [Trot09] mentioned, that technology alliances provided new Research & Development opportunities. However these technological alliances do not always lead to increasing profit within the own Research & Development. Xerox' Palo Alto Research Centre (henceforth.: PARC) determined some technological breakthroughs, on whose they weren't able to profit from their technology. For example they

---

[13] see also: [Murr09]: Borrowing Brilliance - The Six Steps to Business Innovation by Building on the Ideas of Others

[14] see also: [Quot11]: Quote Database

[15] see also: [Trot09]: Why 'Open Innovation' is old wine in new bottles, p. 718 et seq.

determined the graphical-user-interface technology, which became later usage in today's well-known computer mouse. The fourth principle has been investigated by Trott & Hartmann [Trot09] as well. They found out, that being the first on the market doesn't ensure the competitor - victory. In the commencement of personal computer for example, the company Micro Instrumentation and Telemetry Systems (henceforth.: MITS) with their personal computer Altair 8800 as well as Apple with their Apple 2 were the pioneers for the first personal computers. However the first doesn't meant to be the winner. IBM as well as Compaq and Dell dashed on the former personal computer - market just a few years later and won the market race. Another famous example for that can be found within the search engine market. This example clarifies that not the first on the market means to be the winner. Altavista from a DEC - Research Project arrived on the market in 1994 and was the first full text search engine and was the fastest method for finding information on the World Wide Web.[16] Yahoo followed one year later with their search engine 'Yahoo!' and acquired the competitors 'Overture', 'Altavista' and 'AlltheWeb'.[17],[18] Nowadays Page's and Brin's Stanfort Research Project 'Google' is today's market leader with a market share of more than 82%, which is definitively the winner on the search engine market.[19] Like Trott & Hartmann [Trot09] stated: "The pioneer was overhauled by the late entrant that developed a superior algorithm, facilitating more accurate searches." Henry Chebrough [Ches06] believed that, if a company creates the most and best ideas in the industry, then this company will win the competitive-race within the Closed Innovation - paradigm. Even this believe seems to be made up out of thin air. Trott & Hartmann [Trot09] as well as B. Hindo [Hind07] explained that 3M faced a lot of creativity on how to research on technological breakthroughs. However 3M struggled with their efficiency and the captured ideas couldn't be converted into products and services. The sixth and final principle of the Closed Innovation - paradigm which was stated by Henry Chesbrough [Ches06] seems to be unreal as well. The intellectual property of companies which achieved technological breakthroughs has been licenced. 1975 Paul Allen and Bill Gates informed MITS that they got an interpretor for the Altair 8800. The thereupon founded company 'Microsoft' became MITS' general licensor.[20] The sucess of Microsoft today should be adequately known.

---

[16] see also: [Lewi95]: Digital Equipment Offers Web Browsers Its 'Super Spider'

[17] see also: [Whoi11]: Whois Lookup for 'Yahoo.com'

[18] see also: [Pand04]: The death of AltaVista and AlltheWeb

[19] see also: [Netm11]: Search Engine Market Share

[20] see also: [Alla01]: A history of the personal computer: the people and the technology

Summarizing the Closed Innovation - paradigm had always some points, where the companies opened up their boundaries in order to achieve greater Research & Development as well as expansion, which can be indicated as unnamed Open Innovation. However Henry Chesbrough [Ches06] has been the first person who published this paradigm as a solitary method. Nevertheless the "new" method is a well-functioning implant on Research & Development - managers' brains. Furthermore the mutation from Closed Innovation to Open Innovation leads to new opportunities (cf. Figure5) but it leads to new risks as well (cf. Figure6). The Research & Development considerations of the firm need to change in order to stay competitive on the current market. Additionally the satisfaction in the demand for entering new -and other markets have to be clarified as well.

1.3   Bringing Open Innovation to IT Services - the correct implementation of Open Innovation

Traditionally businesses are following Porter's Value Chain of economic activities (cf. Figure 8). This chain is applicable to all processes, which act intending to add value to a product within its lifecycle through the company.[21] In Porter's Value Chain businesses transform input into outputs through a series of processes. Henry Chesbrough [Ches11] stated that the product goes through core manufacturing activities (Inbound logistics, operations, outbound logistics) as well as through supporting manufacturing activities (Other functions, such as procurement and HR). M.E. Porter [Port85] classified these supporting activities like followed:

- Firm Infrastructure
- Human Resources
- Technology Development
- Procurement

Furthermore all the combined activities lead, regarding to M.E. Porter [Port85], to margin.

---

[21] see also: [Ches11]: Bringing Open Innovation to Services, p. 86 et seq.

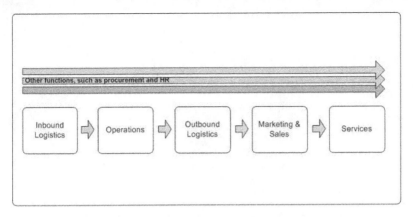

Figure 8: Porter's Value Chain, cf. [Port85] ; [Ches11], p. 86

In Figure 8 customer contacts comes only at the end of the value chain, in the form of 'Services'. In regards to Henry Chesbrough [Ches11], companies like IBM have to face this kind of problem, that most of the companies' revenues take place due to Services. Paul Horn, Senior Vice President of Research at IBM, confirmed this occurence. In regards to Horn, most of todays research activities are geared to support a company that make products, at IBM computer systems, servers, mainframes as well as software. Furthermore Paul Horn stated to Henry Chesbrough [Ches11], that more than half of IBM's revenues resulting in Services. However IBM isn't the only one who face a steadily revenue growth of Services. In regards to the Organisation for Economic co-operation and Development Council [Oecd05] the service sector accounts over 70% of the employees across the Organisation for Economic Co-Operation and Development (henceforth.: OECD) countries, which leads to a globalization of services. Implicating to this issue, [Oecd05] mentioned, that business environments have to be improved for services, in order to strive against barriers to entrepreneurship as well as running businesses. Henry Chesbrough [Ches11] showed up these problematic as well. The traditional value chain (cf. Figure 8) seems to be out of harmony with todays' business environments and their increasing demands for services. Furthermore customer demands changed. Drucker said regarding to Henry Chesbrough [Ches11], that "What the customer buys and considers value is never a product. It is always utility - that is, what a product does for him." Additionally Reichwald & Piller [Reic05] stated, that the innovation processes should be initiated by the customers.

Therefore Henry Chesbrough [Ches11] mentioned Levitt's and Drucker's alternative approach, the so-called 'Service Value Web', (cf. Figure 9), in order to replace Porter's Value Chain for high- service companies.

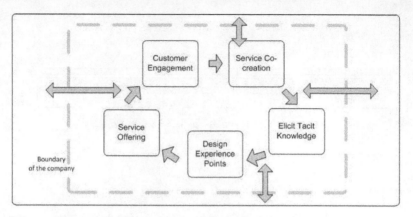

Figure 9: Levitt's and Drucker's 'Service Value Web', cf. [Ches11]

Regarding to Figure9, there is no linear transformation - process from an input to an output. Instead the Service Value Web is a kind of an iterative process which involves customer activities within the process.

Customer interactions, outside the boundaries of the company

Hence companies have more competitors in today's business it is inevitable to implement those customer interactions in form of marketing processes. Those processes should follow the elements of marketing communication (cf. Figure10), determined by Kotler et al. [Kotl05], in order to achieve successful customer implementation into the service value web.

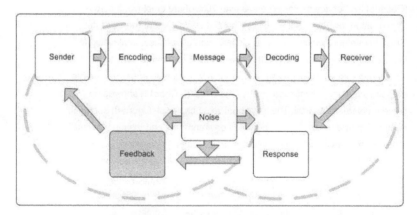

Figure 10: Elements in the marketing communication process, cf. [Kotl05]

Those kind of customer interaction could extend the Figure4 by R&D inputs from the customers (cf. Figure11). Therefore the customer gives like in Figure 10 mentioned Feedback to the company. This feedback could help the Research & Development in order to develop a more fitting product for their markets.

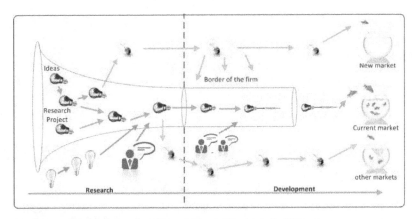

Figure 11: OI - paradigm extended with customer feedback into the R&D, cf. [Ches06], p.25

"Openness generally refers to the ways of sharing with others and inviting their participation".[22] This participation seems to be very important while developing new products. Reichwald & Piller [Reic05] pointed out that there are flop rates of approximately 50%, after launching new products on the markets. These flop rates are caused by the wrong implementations of satisfactions regarding to the customer demands'.[23] Peter Drucker [Druc88] stated, that the key question within the fast changing markets is: How to innovate? In regards to Reichwald & Piller [Reic05] the Open Innovation - paradigm replaces therefore the customer orientation concept by customer integration. Not just Reichwald & Piller [Reic05] stated these changing handling customer. Henry Chesbrough [Ches11] pointed out, that openness refers to the way of sharing with each others as well as inviting their participation within the New Product Development (cf. Chapter 2.2). Furthermore Henry Chesbrough [Ches11] mentioned that there are two complementary ways of openness within the Open Innovation - paradigm, which have been visualized within Figure 12.

---

[22] see also: [Ches11]: Bringing Open Innovation to Services, p. 87 - 88
[23] see also: [Reic05] Open Innovation: Kunden als Partner im Innovationsprozess, p. 2 et seq.

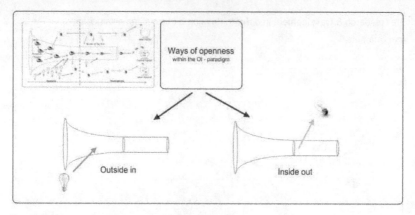

Figure 12: Ways of openness, cf. [Ches11], p. 88 et seq.

In regards to Henry Chesbrough [Ches11] a company has the choice between these two complementary ways of opening (cf. Figure 12). 'Outside in' means, that a company makes a greater use of external ideas and technologies for succeeding their own targets. 'Inside out' is the way, a company allows other businesses the usage of some of their own ideas and / or technologies.

1.3.1 Examples of 'Outside in' and 'Inside out'

The danish company LEGO A/S e.g. used the Outside In approach within their development of the 'Lego Mindstorms'. Henry Chesbrough [Ches11] mentioned that LEGO included programmable motors within their 'Mindstorms'. Someone hacked into the software of the motors to give his robot more functions. However LEGO S/A opened up its software and allowed any kind of modifications. This kind of openness had one great implication. Students were now learning about programming as well as robot design by building LEGO robots. Today there is even a League of such LEGO robots, called the First Lego League (henceforth.: FLL), where robots from all over the world face challenges. Hence students program the robots for their challenges, big companies like National Instruments, Rockwell Automation, 3M as well as Vestas are partners of the FLL.[24] Henry Chesbrough's [Ches11] example for an 'Inside out' openness is about the american internet giant Amazon.com, Inc. who opened up their knowledge and technology. Amazon let retailers use their experience of developing retailer websites. Furthermore Amazon offered these companies the usage of their servers and infrastructure and in some cases the performing of the

---

[24] see also: [Firs11]: First Lego League

fulfillment as well as the merchandising. Thus made Amazon the infrastructure supplier for external companies. Finally Henry Chesbrough [Ches11] stated, that Amazon offers cloud computing services to potential customers. Amazon had great and worthwhile ideas how to get paid for their knowledge and IT services. This was just possible due to the opening up of Amazon's boundaries.

Reichwald & Piller [Reic05] mentioned, that the target of openning should be the usage of creative potential from external sources in order to reduce the risk of Research & Development investments in innovative activities. Therefore Stefan Thomke [Thom03] described two different kinds of information, which a company should consider within their innovation process:

- Need information: Information about the customer as well as the market needs, which could be preferences, wishes, buying motives and satisfaction factors
- Solution Information: describes technological possibilities and potentials. Customer needs should be transformed into a service in an efficient and effective manner.

Implicating to this target, solution information should be added to the innovation process from all over the market. The innovation process should be handled as an interactive relationship between the company and their customers, suppliers and partners.[25] The Open Innovation - paradigm extends the range for finding ideas and solutions. Furthermore Reichwald & Piller [Reic05] stated, that the Open Innovation - paradigm enhances the access to solution information and mentioned that customers have been used too less as a source of external knowledge. These customers are still considered as the value recipients, not as value creator.

1.3.2 Ways to use external knowledge and customers as value creators

"Work closely with customers to develop new solutions". This quotation from Henry Chesbrough [Ches11] shows the problem, which companies have to face. How can customers be implemented in the Research & Development funnel (cf. Figure 2, Figure 4) in order to achieve greater Research & Development power. Referring to Henry Chesbrough [Ches11], IBM is using pilot project to team up with customers in order to solve a particular problem. This agreement has the target, that the outcoming knowledge is shared within the teams. Thus the customer gets a good solution and IBM get the

---

[25] see also: [Reic05]: Open Innovation: Kunden als Partner im Innovationsprozess, p. 5 et seq.

opportunity to reuse the new knowledge with other customers. This approach is used within the IT Mangement of the Daimler AG as well. The IT Management of the Daimler AG operates like an inhouse consulting for their internal customers. The software and services as well as the New Product Development are handled jointly with the customers in order to meet their demand and customer satisfaction.[26] Another IT-service which set the focus on the utility rather than on the product is Xerox. Henry Chesbrough [Ches11] stated that Xerox is offering 'managed print services'. Regarding to what is mentioned before in Figure9, Levitt would say in Xerox' case: People don't want copiers, they want copies. Thus Xerox is offering their customers copies on a fixed price and takes over all activities which are necessary to make copies, which is installing, maintenance, infrastructure management etc. In regards to Henry Chesbrough [Ches11] Xerox' customers save more than 25% on printing and copying costs and Xerox itself gets additional knowledge about their customers' processes.

However there are more ways to use external knowledge and toolkits by using and implementing Web 2.0 technologies combined with the Open Innovation - paradigm. With hindsight the following IT - services, tools or platforms were just possible due to Rasmus Lerdorf's [Lerd11] development of the script language PHP, which is anon adapted from the former languages C and Pearl. Thus it seems, that the borrowing of ideas even within programming language, which was mentioned earlier in this document regarding to David Murray [Murr10], still take place today. Web 2.0 is a collaborative approach, to make user interactions dynamically and interactively. Furthermore Dr. L. Mortara et al. [Mort09] stated, that Open Source Software as well as the Web 2.0 - tools have revolutionized the innovation processes. The users are now able to contribute to innovation, what enhance the openness.[27] The following examples are using such Web 2.0 technologies in order to help the Open Innovation - paradigm come through. Each way have been explained by the usage of examples:

---

[26] see also: [Sigl10]: Eingliederung im Application Management als serviceorientierte Schnittstelle des IT-Management nach der ITIL-Prozessdisziplin SLM.
[27] see also: [Mort09]: How to implement open innovation

Usage of Open-Source-Communities: Reichwald & Piller [Reic05] mentioned, that many big companies implemented organisational structures in order to use communities. Furthermore the way of community working gave start-up's totally new opportunities. Famous examples are the MySQL developers as well as the Luxembourg voice over IP company Skype Ltd. Both are developing their products on the basis of the market need's.[28]

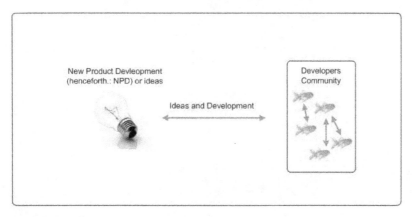

New Product Devleopment
(henceforth.: NPD) or ideas

Ideas and Development

Developers
Community

Figure 13: Open Source functionality

Referring to Figure 13 the development of Open-Source Software takes place, while the users conceptualize the systems within a 'Community'. Therefore the users work collaborative. All users work at the same time on the same new product or idea but on different parts of the project. Hence ideas of users can be used by other users their work or activities can be enhanced. Furthermore such a community can create their own development environment, e.g. the Software Development Kit Eclipse. Open Source community projects like Linux or Apache-Web-Server have been developed in such a way. Nowadays these products are not just niche products of computer nerds, it's quite the opposite. The latest 'Web Server Survey' from Matt Foster [Fost11] showed, that Apache has the highest increase with 11.4M hostnames of overall 14.7M new hostnames. Thus makes Apache the most used mass product with a market percentage of 61,13% followed by Microsoft with 18,83%.[29] However a lot of companies are using Open-Source-Software as a basis for their commercialized software. This means, that they are using external knowledge of communities in order to bring their product on a commercialized way on the market. The german systems engineer 'abas systems gmbh' is selling a document management system, called HABEL. HABEL's kernel is based on Open Source Software. When a customer needs to find a document, he has to use the search engine. This search engine is based on Open Source

---

[28] see also: [Reic05]: Open Innovation: Kunden als Partner im Innovationsprozess, p. 6
[29] see also: [Fost11]: Web Server Survey

code. Basically abas isn't commercializing the Open Source Software, but the necessary add-on's and plugin's.[30] This example shows, that companies can use external knowledge and technology breakthroughs in order to expand their own IT-services. However Julian Birkinshaw et al. [Birk11] pointed out that communities like online forums are not a panacea for innovation.

---

[30] see also: [Abas11]: HABEL Dokumentenmanagement & eBusiness

Feedback platforms: Reichwald & Piller [Reic05] described them as "Toolkits for User Innovation". Therefore companies can use different ways to interact with the customers in the Research & Development - New Product Development (cf. Figure 14).

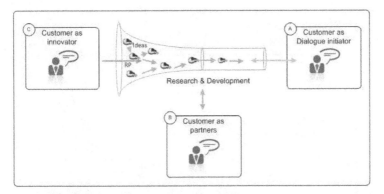

Figure 14: Three ways of Customer Interaction, cf. [Reic05]

Referring to Figure 14, customers can participate in three different ways. "A" they can initiate a dialogue with manufacturers, "B" they could be equal partners of the organization or "C" they could act as independent innovators, which would be the most open way of customer interaction.[31] These kind of customer interaction could be just possible due to the before mentioned collaboration element 'Web 2.0 ', which expands the World Wide Web with interactive Web Services. The user integration can take place in two different ways, which are visualized in Figure 15.

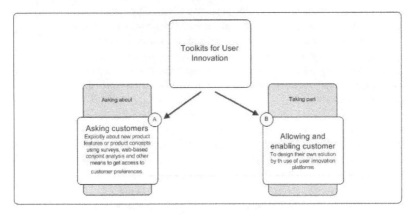

Figure 15: Toolkits for User Innovation, cf. [Reic05], p.9 et seq.

---

[31] see also: [Reic05]: Open Innovation: Kunden als Partner im Innovationsprozess

Technology marketplace: If a company has a problem or a need for an idea, they can ask companies like Innocentive and Innovaro to publish an announcement on their technology marketplace, what is pointed out with point A and B on Figure16. Then the announcements reach their clients, which are external innovators in order to solve technological issues over the internet. The best answers or ideas will receive a reward, which could go till 100.000 Dollar.[32]

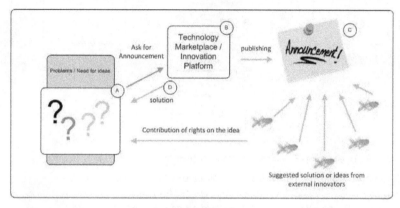

Figure 16: Processes for a technology marketplace.

In regards to Frank Piller [Pill06] the innovator has to contribute the rights to the company, who searched an idea or answer. Additionally the company itself pays a charge to the innovation platform. Frank Piller [Pill06] , co-director of the MIT Smart Customizing Group, believes that this model implicates strong opportunities for the fast usage of external innovations. However Julian Birkinshaw et al. [Birk11] pointed out, that the number of responses could be very low, but the one submitted response e.g. a Roche Diagnostics, issue was brilliant. Furthermore such innovation platforms or technology marketplaces "highlight the value of tapping into external group".[33] Referring to Frank Piller [Pill06] the educational background of such innovators can be completely different. However over the half of the innovators have a PhD degree. Innovation platforms are not seeking to address the customers or product users of the different companies, what makes it a different approach than communities. The target group is, regarding to Frank Piller [Pill06], a wide group of knowledge carriers. For these knowledge carriers it would be more lucrative to secure their ideas with a patent. However Karim Lakhani [Lakh00] found out, that a lot of those innovators found a solution after a few days, what implicates that the solutions are based on former issues. Not just only Innocentive is operating such a platform. Companies with other target groups are e.g. NineSigma, who tries to find experts of the respective scopes. Frank Piller [Pill06] stated,

---

[32] see also: [Pill06]: Produktentwicklung mit Hilfe der Web-Community
[33] see also: [Birk11]: The 5 Myths of Innovation, p.47

that NineSigma as contrasted with Innocentive, doesn't want to find solutions, they try to find ideas which could lead to solutions of certain issues. Another innovation platform is YourEncore, whose innovators are retired scientists, who can hired within a short-term agreement. Ideacrossing e.g. is launching, the so-called idea competitions with the customers. Referring to others it seems to be a special case, because Ideacrossing is the only innovation platform, who is implementing the customers within the innovation process. Therefore the earlier mentioned rules (cf Figure 9,Figure 10, Figure 11) should apply for this company. In regards to Frank Piller [Pill06], the German HyveAG seems to be a successful producer of such innovation platforms. Therefor the HyveAG is offering customized products and helps the customers within all the development chain of the platform. Furthermore it seems, that the HyveAG is using the OI - paradigm on it's own by setting the customer as the omphalos of the project. Therefore the focus of each developed innovation platform were on the customers needs.[34]

---

[34] see also: [Hyve11]: Customized Innovation - Vom Fuzzy Frontend bis zur Markteinführung

Customer Survey: The implementation of the customers as an input into the Research & Development chain has a big advantage regarding to approaches like innovation platforms. Customer survey's are more or less costless.[35]

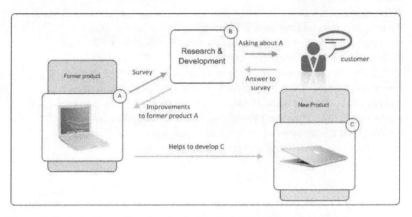

Figure 17: Customer Survey for enhancing the Research & Development, cf. [Pill06]

Frank Piller [Pill06] mentioned the German automobile supplier Webasto, who is using customer survey's in order to improve their products, which will be implemented in many different cars. Therefore they are asking actual drivers of these cars in their former versions. Of course these customer survey's need to follow the before mentioned method, how to implement the customers into the innovation funnel.

Finally Frank Piller [Pill06] mentioned, that the character of the internal Research & Development is changing while implementing external innovators. Quality Assurance, enhancements as well as the transfer from innovative concepts into the stage of industrial application are the new focus of internal Research & Development hence they are using external knowledge and ideas.

Summarizing Levitt's and Drucker's Service Value Web (cf. Figure9) seems to be the right approach for a opened up Research & Development process within the IT-service sector. Thus the Service Value Web with the customer or innovator implementation is replacing Porter's Value Chain. Furthermore we recognized, that the customer is demanding the utility of a product, rather than the product itself. Henry Chesbrough [Ches11] mentioned that providing the customer a real value instead of just the product, makes them less likely to switch to competitors. This could be considered as a competitive advantage. Therefore a company is able to gain competitive

---

[35] see also: [Pill06]: Produktentwicklung mit Hilfe der Web-Community

advantage due to the right implementation of customers. However for these implementation it is necessary to evaluate, how to get the right information (cf. Figure 10, Figure 11) in order to improve the New Product Development within the Research & Development. The 'openness' of the firm boundaries can be, regarding to Henry Chesbrough [Ches11], established through two different ways, 'Outside in' and 'Inside out'. In regards to Julian Birkinshaw et al. [Birk11] "the Web 2.0 - technologies have made it possible to democratize the process even further, and offer ways of consolidating and evaluating radically new ideas". Henceforth the before mentioned Web 2.0 - technology tools, who help using external knowledge as well as ideas seems to foster the Open Innovation - paradigm on it's successful way. But these online tools, open innovation communities and big collaborative forums have their limitations.[36] Referring to Julian Birkinshaw et al. [Birk11] the implementation of such Web 2.0 - technologies involves carful judgement and a deep understanding of the challenges which have to be faced by a company. However the Web 2.0 breakthrough accelerate Open Innovation - tools like communities or forums. Even the of Julian Birkinshaw et al. [Birk11] mentioned, McKinsey survey, that the Web 2.0 tools just got a 21% satisfaction of the users and on the other hand a dissatisfaction of 22% cannot dampen the enthusiasm. Furthermore it seems, that the implementation of an Open Innovation - paradigm triggers learning skills between companies and their customers. These learning skills are based on such Web 2.0 - tools as well. Learning and knowledge exchange are defined as basic activities within the innovation process.[37] In order to anticipate the enthusiasm of companies, Julian Birkinshaw et al. [Birk11] mentioned that the Open Innovation - paradigm should be implemented supplemental, not solitary.

---

[36] see also: [Birk11]: The 5 Myths of Open Innovation, p.45 et seq.

[37] see also: [Reic05]: Open Innovation: Kunden als Partner im Innovationsprozess, p.6 et seq.

2

Affectation of Open Innovation to the Business Development

In Chapter 1, the Open Innovation - paradigm has been differentiated from the traditional, Closed Innovation - paradigm. Furthermore it has been pointed out, that the implementation of the Open Innovation - paradigm lead to new opportunities within the Research & Development of an organization. Additionally the integration of the Open Innovation - paradigm has been evaluated with the conclusion, that it doesn't seem to be a totally new approach. However it have been stated, that the Open Innovation - paradigm shouldn't been implemented solitary. By showing a string of examples, it has been determined, how the Open Innovation - paradigm have been adapted within the IT Service industry. Examples where comprised of Web2.0 tools (cf. Chapter1.3.2).

Hence the first two subproblems or subquestions (cf. page6, Question 1, Question 2) of the thesis have been evaluated and adressed, this chapter has to determine, if there is a relationship between the implementation of Open Innovation and the Business Development. Furthermore it should be pointed out, how a possible relationship has been taken place in three determined companies. In order to achieve a complete overview, the field of Business Development has to be, first of all, defined and integrated.

2.1   Definition and Integration of the Business Development

2.1.1 Definition of the Business Development

In regards to Andrew Greta [Gret08], Business Development means different things to different organizations and summarized the different thoughts. For some it could be described as landing new business from new customers, for others generating new and continued businesses from existing customers, or it just can be described as a discipline charged with driving corporate growth, what Tom Lautenbacher [Laut11] agreed.[38] The integration of the Business Development can be described by using Ansoff's [Anso65] model of strategic planning. The model is, regarding to Georg Angermeier [Ange07] based on 4 parts, which are further showed up within Figure18 :

- market penetration
- market development
- product development
- diversification

---

[38] see also: [Gret08]: What is Business Development?

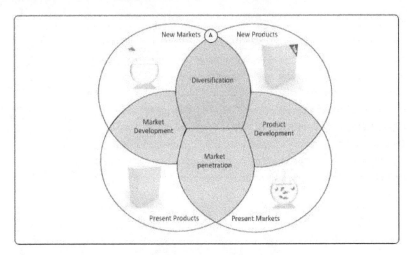

Figure 18: Altered Ansoff-Matrix, la./ cf. [Anso65] & [Gret08]

Point A on Figure18 is therefore the range, what have to be processed and adressed within the Business Development. Hence it can be described as the overlap between the activities for reaching both, new markets as well as the activities in order to launch new products on those markets. Comparing to Andrew Greta [Gret08] , Figure 19 have been created for completing the organizational overview by field of businesses. Like demonstrated with Figure 18 before, the field of Business Development would be Point C of the following figure.

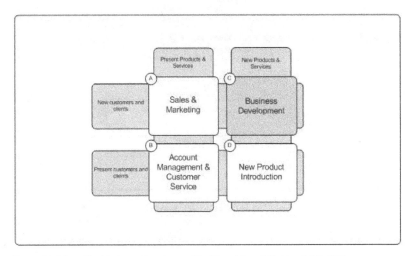

Figure 19: Integration Business Development in Altered Ansoff-Matrix, cf. [Gret08]

Referring to Figure 18 and Figure 19, Business Development is referring to creating both, new customers / clients (new markets) as well as new products / services, which are needed to reach these new customers and clients and to get the business growing with an expanding reach. Henry Chesbrough [Ches06] stated, that alternative paths to the Market increase the possible Business Development. This alternative paths can be created, regarding to Henry Chesbrough [Ches06] due to the implementation of the Open Innovation - paradigm (cf. Chapter 1.2).[39] Figure 20 show up the fragmentation which is used within this dissertation to explain the usage of Open Innovation within the Business Development.

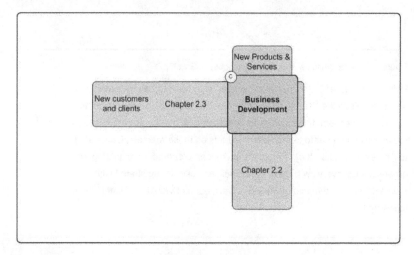

Figure 20: Fragmentation of the Business Development

[39] see also [Ches06]: Open Innovation - The New Imperative for Creating and Profiting from Technology

2.2   Open Innovation in the New Product Development

2.2.1 The Evolution of Research & Development

To understand the impact of the Open Innovation integration into the
Business Development, the historical process from the Invention and
Commercialization generation till the Research & Development generation
should be mentioned: As far back as 1943 Joseph Schumpeter [Schu43]
emphasis "the fundamental impulse that sets and keeps the capitalist engine
in motion comes from the new consumers' goods, the new methods of
production or transportation, the new markets, the new forces of industrial
organisation that capitalist enterprise creates." The Question therefore is,
which role the Open Innovation -paradigm could play within the
Development of new products and services?

First of all, Innovation seems to be a successful realization of something
"new" on the market.[40] Serhan Ili [Sili09] stated, that since the
industrialization there are research abilities on processes as well as
methods in order to improve the new product development, what is one of
the in Figure 18, Figure 19 and Figure 20 mentioned cores of the Business
Development. The following 4-phase model (cf. Figure 21), regarding to
helps, McGrath [Mcgr04], to illustrate the changes within the product
development.

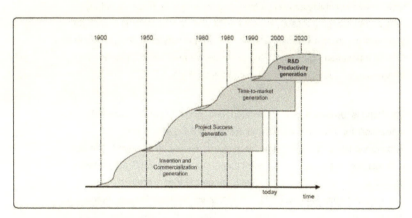

Figure 21: Product Development phases, cf. [Mcgr04] ; [Sili09], p.18

Serhan Ili [Sili09] mentioned, that Research & Development occured the first
time 1887 in WestOrange/USA, when Thomas Edison established the first
Research & Development - laboratory. This laboratory has been

---

[40] see also [Sili09]: Open Innovation im Kontext der Integrierten Produktentwicklung
Strategien zur Steigerung der FuE Produktivität, p.17 et seq.

implemented due to the activity-focus on inventions as well as advancements of technical solutions and their transformation into valuable, innovative products. McGrath [Mcgr04] added, that approximately 50 years later all important companies had implemented such a Research & Development laboratory. However regarding to Serhan Ili [Sili09] these early Research & Development laboratories generated knowledge exclusively inside and has been used in order to develop new products as well as generating a competitive advantage.

2.2.2 The trend of the new product development

Nowadays the marginal benefits of time reduction within the product development are achieved or even exceeded for a lot of areas. Regarding to Serhan Ili [Sili09] there is an increasing cost as well as innovation pressure, which lead to a reorientation of the product development. Furthermore this reorientation is accelerated by external conditions, like depletion of trade barriers and sinking transaction costs. These conditions which arose due to the globalization lead to an increasingly amount of competitiveness. Companies have to face several challenges like the integration of complex technologies and shorten innovation cycles.[41] Serhan Ili [Sili09] stated that for the accomplishment of such challenges, organizations need to improve their innovation ability as well as changing the way how to create value. Henry Chesbrough [Ches06] stated, that "if you want something done right, you have got to do it yourself" and pointed out the way of working within the Closed Innovation - paradigm. Due to the before mentioned changed, Chesbroughs' quotation is receding into the background.

The trend is towards a product development, which integrates external innovation impulses into the internal Research & Development. Simultaneously a maximum amount of results should be achieved. The aim is to increase the Research & Development productivity. McGrath [Mcgr04] as well as Henry Chesbrough [Ches06] recommended a product development outside organizations' boundaries, because the own resources as well as competences formed within the Research & Development departments have to face limits. Hence that, organizations should hark back to external expertise. This recourse brings Figure 4 again on the agenda. Incoming information, knowledge and technologies lead to an enhancement of Research Projects as well as internal ideas (cf. Chapter 1). This additional

---

[41] see also [Sili09]: Open Innovation im Kontext der Integrierten Produktentwicklung Strategien zur Steigerung der FuE Produktivität, p.23 et seq.

values help the Research & Development department to develop new products with new technologies or ideas within their Research & Development funnel (cf. Chapter 1). These new products can be launched on the current market and enhance therefore the Business Development.

For illustration purposes the assumption, that no Research & Development scientists leave the organization with their gained knowledge as well as ideas is anticipated. Thus it would be a perfect implementation of the Open Innovation - paradigm for developing new products.

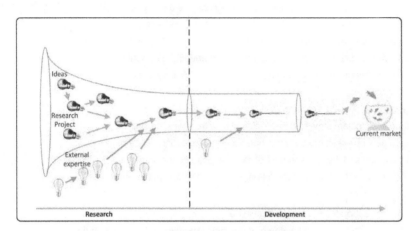

Figure 22: Own figure - Open Innovation in New Product Development 1, cf. [Reic06] , [Ches06]

Flow of Research Projects and ideas within the boundary / border of the company / organization

Ideas or Research Projects are starting outside the companies boundaries / borders and move into the Research & Development funnel

External Expertise could be, regarding to Henry Chesbrough [Ches06]: external Research Projects, Venture investing, technology in-licensing or technology acquisition. Furthermore incoming scientists could be an external expertise as well. However such a implementation of the Open Innovation - paradigm seems, regarding to Figure 22, to lead to competitive advantage, due to incoming External expertise and no outgoing information or knowledge.

2.3 Open Innovation for getting New Customers / Clients

Henry Chesbrough [Ches06] stated the example, that Lucent enabled the Bell Labs in order to make research on new technologies. Afterwards Lucent realized the potential of these labs in their own business and explored how to do more with the labs as well as their research talents. "Out of this exploration emerged Lucent's New Ventures Group".[42] Therefore the New Ventures Group was created in order to commercialize the new technologies which were found within the Bell Laboratories, which belongs today to Alcatel-Lucent.[43] The Bell Laboratories describes its own, regarding to Alcatel - Lucent [Alca11] as "where vision and technology meet our customers' needs". However Henry Chesbrough [Ches06] mentioned, that Lucent conducted extensive external benchmarking. This should helped them in determining how to finance their new technology ventures. The results were, that benchmarks with other companies like Xerox, 3M or Intel occured. However regarding to Henry Chesbrough [Ches06], Lucent had to face the problem, how to commercialize new technologies and finally build up a new business model which balanced the protection of internal innovation and the development of external paths to the market. Furthermore this business model helped Lucent's internal Business Development.[44]

The Bell Laboratories are well-known due to its explorations of the Unix operating system as well as the programming language "C", what has been developed in order to program Unix.[45]

In regards to Henry Chesbrough [Ches06], external incoming ideas or technologies can motivate a company to get these ideas faster to the market, what Frank Mattes [Matt11] agreed. A faster-to-the-market approach implicates faster feedback from the market and hence, faster learning for the Research & Development within the organization itself. This kind of environment could lead, regarding to Henry Chesbrough [Ches06] to a competitive advantage, due to learning faster and performing more capable. The combination of own products with external information or ideas could lead to new and useful products and services.[46] Like David Murray [Murr09]

---

[42] see also: [Ches06] Open Innovation - The New Imperative for Creating and Profiting from Technology, p.135 et seq.

[43] see also: [Alca11]: Alcatel-Lucent - Bell Labs

[44] see also: [Ches06]: Open Innovation - The New Imperative for Creating and Profiting from Technology, p.135 et seq.

[45] see also: [Ward10]: 40 years of Unix

[46] see also: [Ches06] Open Innovation - The New Imperative for Creating and Profiting from Technology, p.135 et seq.

already mentioned, the borrowing of others' ideas is a good way to achieve something new (new products/services) and a, regarding to Henry Chesbrough [Ches06] "powerful way to create value". Hence new products may apply to launch on new markets or on the market of others' , Figure 23 can be adjusted to the following, which implicates the reach of new customers or clients:

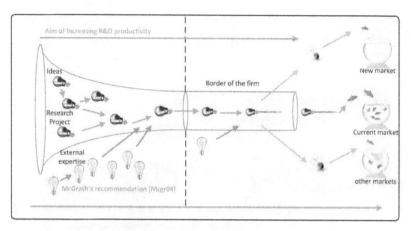

Figure 23: Own figure - Open Innovation in New Product Development 2, cf. [Reic06] , [Ches06], [Mcgr04]

Flow of Research Projects and ideas within the boundary / border of the company / organization

Flow of new products onto new market due to integrated external information and knowledge in the own Research & Development funnel

Flow of new products onto other markets due to integrated external information and knowledge in the own Research & Development funnel

Ideas or Research Projects are starting outside the companies boundaries / borders and move into the Research & Development funnel

New product which grow up from innovation are, regarding to Hans-Dieter Zollondz [Zoll05], products with totally new prospects. Furthermore they are the most essential part for competitiveness.[47] For the necessary communication with the customers in order to merchandise the developed,

---

[47] see also: [Zoll05]: Marketing - Mix - Die sieben P's des Marketings

enhanced or new products on new- or other markets, the communication principles (cf. Figure 10) need to apply therefore as well. Hence a fast to the market implies a fast feedback from the customer. A faster feedback itself is enhancing the Research & Development funnel and therefore the fast to the market approach.

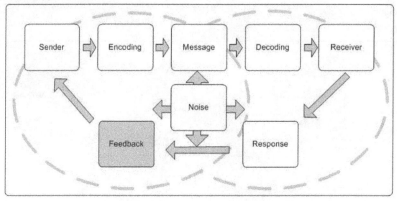

Figure 24: Copy of Figure10

However we assumed in Figure 22 and Figure 23, that no scientist leave the organization with their gained knowledge or experience. In reality we would come back to the in Figure 4 showed assumption. However Figure22 and Figure 23 helped to illustrate the two Business Development determinations. Like already mentioned before, internal scientists are able to leave the boundaries of the company in order to create a start-up. This start-up can be acquired later to come back into the firm boundaries'. However a company should maintain their scientists and employees to get a Research & Development funnel like mentioned in Figure 23.

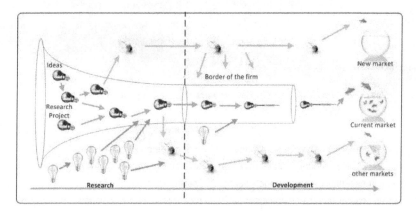

Figure 25: Copy of Figure 4

2.4 Relationship of Open Innovation and the Business Development, a survey shows the implementation in practice

2.4.1 The aim of the survey

The survey has been prepared in order to point out the relationship between the Business Development, which was mentioned in Chapter 2.1 and the implementation of the in Chapter 1 mentioned Open Innovation - paradigm. The findings and outcomes of this survey cannot be described as empirical studies, because the determined companies are just a small collection of inquiries. Furthermore the outcomes cannot be considered as representing facts for whole industries or businesses, due to a minor scope of investigation. However the results show up a direction, which further investigations could address and enhance with empirical analysis and studies.

2.4.2 The samples of the survey

The following information are based on a survey, which had been answered first by Dr. Volker Nestle, Director of Microsystems / Research and Innovation from the German company Festo AG & Co. KG, second by Georg Boag, CEO of the Scottish company Targeting Innovation Ltd and third by Dr. Detlef Kirsch, Interim Manager from the German company Engineering + Innovation.

Festo is a company for control, and automation technologies, Targeting Innovation Ltd. is an innovation consultancy who is developing web based project management services with the usage of the in Chapter 1.3.2 mentioned Web 2.0 - technologies. Engineering + Innovation is an Interims Management company which is specialized on competencies in innovation management, favoring the implementation of Open Innovation.[48],[49]

2.4.3 Usage of Open Innovation within the Business Development

All three investigated companies use the Open Innovation - paradigm for the in Chapter 1 mentioned reasons of implementing. Festo is using the approach for their lead user integration, for research networks, customer & supplier workshops as well as for web based technology platforms (probably

---

[48] see also: [Boag11]: Survey about the relationship between Open Innovation and the Business Development
[49] see also: [Kirs11]: Survey about the relationship between Open Innovation and the Business Development

the in Chapter 1.3.2 mentioned Web 2.0 - tools).[50] Targeting Innovation is using the approach in order to find new intellectual property as well as new business opportunities by using resources like the Enterprise Europe Network as well as their own contacts. Furthermore Targeting Innovation is considering to license their own intellectual property to other organizations.[51] Thus is a similar approach like the in Chapter 1.3.1 mentioned example of Amazon.com and would be a great opportunity for the company in order to get value out of their knowledge. Engineering + Innovation is using the Open Innovation - paradigm in order to gain additional know-how from their customers, external partners like universities and institutions as well as suppliers, technologies and even by benchmarking with their competitors.

All of the three companies can recognize improvements within their Business Development after the implementation of the Open Innovation - paradigm into their Research & Development funnel. Dr. Volker Nestle [Nest11] recognize strong improvements especially in the new business fields, what point out, that the Business Development seems to get enhanced, due to the Open Innovation (cf. Chapter 2.2, Chapter 2.3). This enhancement take place due to the use and integration of external competencies for new products ans new sales channels (New markets, due to new customers / clients, cf. Chapter 2.3) as well as selling intellectual property and knowledge to external partner. Thus Festo is using both, "Outside In" as well as "Inside Out" approaches (cf. Chapter 1.3).[52] Georg Boag [Boag11] mentioned, that Targeting Innovation gets business development opportunities through signpostings as well as collaborative bids for research funding or more specific business opportunities. Therefore they are using fundings like the Seventh Framework Programme, FP7 from the European Commission, CORDIS.[53] This alterations to the Business Development of Targeting Innovation take place due to the ensuring that the business development staff can explore new opportunities through their innovation network. Dr. Detlef Kirsch [Kirs11] mentioned, that due to the implementation of the Open Innovation - paradigm, Engineering + Innovation is able to generate significant growth in business for selected products as well as market segments. Furthermore they are able to get a temporarily monopoly for their key products, due to the implementation of external

---

[50] see also: [Nest11]: Survey about the relationship between Open Innovation and the Business Development
[51] see also: [Boag11]: Survey about the relationship between Open Innovation and the Business Development
[52] see also: [Nest11]: Survey about the relationship between Open Innovation and the Business Development
[53] see also: [Cord11]: European Commission CORDIS - Seventh Framework Programme

knowledge. Additionally Dr. Detlef Kirsch [Kirs11] stated, that they file patents for technologies, what lead them into a cost leadership position. Thus the Open Innovation - paradigm "improved and accelerated their brainstorming as well as the evaluation of feasibility studies and the selection of projects leading to more competitiveness in Business Developement." [54] Furthermore all of the three samples, Dr. Volker Nestle [Nest11], Georg Boag [Boag11] as well as Dr. Detlef Kirsch [Kirs11] believe, that there are impacts on knowledge- and information improvements since the implementation of Open Innovation. Dr. Detlef Kirsch [Kirs11] pointed a further development of core competencies and their knowledge data base out. Georg Boag [Boag11] agreed and mentioned, that they received a broader spectrum of expertise to call on.

2.4.4 Competitive Advantage due to the implementation of Open Innovation

Georg Boag [Boag11] pointed out, that the implementation of the Open Innovation - paradigm "brings competitive advantage through new products and processes."[55] Dr. Detlef Kirsch [Kirs11] agreed and added, that Open Innovation generates sustainable growth in business and market share, e.g. by entering or developing emerging / global markets or new business areas. Dr. Volker Nestle [Nest11] thought broader and mentioned, that technological innovation relies, due to increasing complexity, on the effective and efficient combination of distributed resources as well as integrative capabilities. Furthermore he mentioned, that the firms are barely able to allocate all innovation - related assets by themselves. "Complexity has rather led to a cumulative interconnectedness of varying players along the innovation process. This trend goes along with an accelerated diffusion of knowledge due to an increasing availability of knowledge and a higher mobility of individuals. Hence, in terms of sustainability, to maintain or even expand competitiveness, location factors increasingly gain importance beyond a firms own resources and capabilities".[56]

Hence New Products and New Markets are key factors of the Business Development per definition (cf. Chapter 2.1.1, Figure 19), the implementation of an Open Innovation - paradigm into an organizations' Research & Development funnel seems to enhance the Business

---

[54] see also: [Kirs11]: Survey about the relationship between Open Innovation and the Business Development
[55] see also: [Boag11]: Survey about the relationship between Open Innovation and the Business Development
[56] see also: [Nest11]: Survey about the relationship between Open Innovation and the Business Development

Development. This enhancement take place due to a more competitive New Product Development (cf. Chapter 2.1). Not just Dr. Volker Nestle, Georg Boag & Dr. Detlef Kirsch believe, that the implementation of Open Innovation will cause to competitive advantage. The Open Innovation Center (henceorth.: OIC) of the Industrial Technology Research Institute (henceforth.: ITRI) ,Taiwan stated, that the implementation of the Open Innovation -paradigm cause a gain of competitive advantage in global markets, due to collaborating with other organizations in carrying out Research & Development activities and developing innovative Research & Development skills in advanced technologies.[57] Furthermore Malcolm Skingle [Skin09] stated, that Open Innovation allow better access to science & technology, which could lead to competitive advantage as well. Collaborations with Research Institutes as well as Universities promote greater transparency & transfer of ideas. [58]

Summarizing Business Development is focused on the development of two areas, new customers, new products / services. It seems that the usage of the Open Innovation - paradigm helps to enhance both of these areas. However the new product development can be easier enhanced than the creation of new customers, which should be more or less a core competency of the Marketing - field. However the not representive company survey's showed up, that the Open Innovation - paradigm is well used in order to enhance and improve the Business Development and the reach of their businesses. Additionally the implementation entail a competitive advantage compared to other competitors. However there is no source, which determine that Open Innovation is a panacea for a consistent company growth, but it seems that it could help achieving some of the Business Development's targets.

---

[57] see also: [Itri11]: Services of ITRI: Open Innovation Centre
[58] see also: [Skin09]: Achieving competitive advantage through Open Innovation

3

A cul-de-sac of costs and competitive advantage - How Open Innovation cause two snowball - effects

In Chapter 2, the Business Development has been defined and integrated in an organizational overview of departments. One outcome was, that the Business Development take its focus on both, getting new customers/clients (new markets) as well as launching new products/services. Furthermore it has determined, how the Open Innovation - paradigm could affect these key factors (cf. Chapter 2.3, Chapter 2.4) of the Business Development. Additionally it has been pointed out, how competitive advantage can be achieved. Finally a survey helped to show up the implementation of the Open Innovation - paradigm in an Interim Management company and an consultancy which handles with the in Chapter 1 mentioned Web 2.0 - based software (cf. Chapter 1.3.2).

So far the first four subproblems or subquestions (cf. page 6, Question 1, Question 2, Question 3 and Question 4) of the thesis have been addressed and evaluated. This chapter has to determine, if the mutation from the Closed Innovation - paradigm to the Open Innovation - paradigm could lead to an inevitable snowball effect (cf. page 6, Question 5).

Hence there seems to be no literary evidence about the affections of the implementation of Open Innovation as a snowball effect, the following results are based on thoughts, interviews as well as the before mentioned survey. These thoughts are partially implications of the determined results from Chapter 1 and Chapter 2.

3.1 Explanation of the snowball - effect

A snowball - effect is colloquial a self - enhancing process, which had been observed in the nature. Such observations take place, regarding to David Murray [Murr09] since the Stone Age and are important ways of finding solutions for something. The best explanation is, like the name already implies, the example of the snowball, which is rolling down the slope of a mountain. In the beginning a snowball is small. Earth's gravitational force pulls the snowball down till it reach the vale. On its way down the slope, the snowball increase its own mass due to rolling over the snow pack. Since the snow of the snow pack grips on the snowball, the snowball expeditiously could amplify its own size, mass and therefore the speed of rolling. Finally such a rolling-down snowball mutate to a dangerous object or lead to avalanche outbreaks. This effect has been visualized by the following figure:

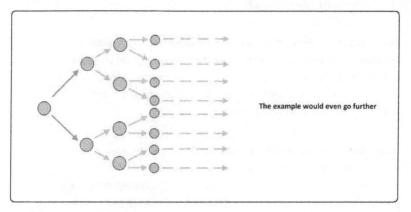

Figure 26: Process of a snowball effect

Within this dissertation, it should be demonstrated, how such a colloquial snowball - effect could take place due to the implementation of the Open Innovation - paradigm in the Business Development.

3.2 Possible snowball - effects due to the implementation of Open Innovation within the Business Development

3.2.1 A cul-de-sac of costs

Alexander Schroll [Schr09] mentioned in his survey about the Research & Development costs, that after the implementation of the Open Innovation - paradigm neither lower nor higher costs can be determined for the Research & Development. However Clemens Frowein [Frow11] believes, that the implementation of the Open Innovation paradigm can be cost intensive. Therefore the most of the costs occur during the implementation at the so-called learning curve.[59]

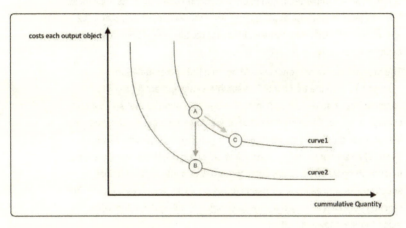

Figure 27 Learning curve, cf. [Pind09]

Economies of scale, more output

Learning effect with sinking costs at the same output. Occur due to the increasing knowledge

Referring to Pindyck & Rubinfeld [Pind09] , the blue arrow in Figure 27, visualize an increase of learning of the usage of a method / approach, which would be in this example the implementation of Open Innovation within the Research & Development funnel. In regards to Clemens Frowein [Frow11] such a learning curve has to be steep in order to achieve sinking costs. However this achievement is a hard job within today's organizational structures. Clemens Frowein [Frow11] believe that the organizational

---

[59] see also: [Frow11]: Virtuelle Weiterentwicklung - Hochschule Heilbronn - Forschungsprojekt 2011

structures are too complex in order to achieve a steep learning curve. Furthermore the implementation of the Open Innovation - paradigm need a change in the minds of the people, what Frank Mattes [Matt11] , Dr.Detlef Kirsch [Kirs11] as well as Dr. Volker Nestle [Nest11] agreed.[60] Therefore Dr. Detlef Kirsch [Kirs11] mentioned in the company survey, that there must be an innovation spirit and a lived innovation process, which need to be supported by the management as well in order to allow people room for new ideas. That would lead to a great impact on the Research & Development processes as well as future investments.[61] Dr. Volker Nestle [Nest11] added, that a the basic problem is not an organizational one. He added, that the implementation is a question of corporate culture.[62] Not just the learning curve, even the implementation of outside technologies or ideas imply costs. The usage of technology marketplaces like Innocentive, cf. Chapter 1.3.2, are regarding to Clemens Frowein [Frow11] cost-intensive implementations of Open Innovation.

The implying snowball - effect would be, that the implementation of Open Innovation within the traditional Research & Development funnel, like described in Chapter 1, is cost intensive due to organizational and corporate cultural changes. Once implemented, there could be a cul-de-sac, because the return to the traditional approach is, regarding to Dr. Volker Nestle [Nest11] might not be helpful, and could be expensive. However if the Open Innovation approach is totally implemented wrong into organizational structures as well as peoples' minds, costs could increase dramatically. This reaction could act like such a snowball, which is rolling down the slope, triggering the snowball - effect.

A possible way to prevent the triggering of this snowball - effect is, not to totally open-up the firm-boundaries. Therefore the Open Innovation - paradigm can be implemented additionally to the traditional Research & Development funnel. Ralf Reichwald & Frank Piller [Reic05] mentioned, that Open Innovation is a encouraging supplementation to actual Research & Development departments. However this doesn't mean the totally abolishment of traditional, company - driven innovation processes. Instead they can be considered as supplementary instruments as well as thought impetus. [63]

---

[60] see also: [Frow11]: Virtuelle Weiterentwicklung - Hochschule Heilbronn - Forschungsprojekt 2011

[61] see also: [Kirs11]: Survey about the relationship between Open Innovation and the Business Development

[62] see also: [Nest11]: Survey about the relationship between Open Innovation and the Business Development

[63] see also: [Reic05]: Open Innovation: Kunden als Partner im Innovationsprozess, p. 13 & 14

3.2.2 Competitive Advantage and effects on competitors

Clemens Frowein [Frow11] picked up the before mentioned way to prevent the snowball - effect. He mentioned, that expensive researchers can be supplemented by the buying-in and networking. Furthermore Frowein [Frow11] stated that this could lead to an increasing potential and to new opportunities in order to achieve competitive advantage. Furthermore he believes, that without the implementation of the Open Innovation - paradigm, companies cannot be competitive in the future. This implies, that the Open Innovation - paradigm should be implemented in the right manner in order to act competitive on the market. First of all a company has to be careful in order not to stuck the first snowball - effect, cf. Chapter 3.2.1. However Georg Boag [Boag11] stated in the company survey his believe, that Open Innovation cause competitive advantage through the causing of new products and new processes. Dr. Detlef Kirsch [Kirs11] agreed to this believe and stated that "Open Innovation generate sustainable growth in business and market share, e.g. by entering or developing emerging / global markets or new business areas." Dr. Volker Nestle [Nest11] agreed, that competitors could implement the Open Innovation - paradigm as well in order to achieve success and competitiveness. However he added, that "each Open Innovation project needs openness from all participants".[64] Therefore Research & Developments departments of Open Innovation associates should be, regarding to Dr. Volker Nestle [Nest11], open to a certain level.

The snowball - effect within the aim of achieving competitive advantage is the fact, that once implemented Open Innovation in order to bring new- or improved products on the markets, the competitors could change their innovation - processes as well. Dr. Detlef Kirsch [Kirs11] stated, that their competency network with technology partners as well as competitors would change their Research & Development as well in order to stay competitive. Therefore Georg Boag [Boag11] agreed the question if competitors would change to the Open Innovation approach just with a simple "Yes" and Dr. Volker Nestle [Nest11] agreed to this question as well.[65] These findings point out, that if an organization is implementing the Open Innovation - paradigm in order to enhance their Business Development, their competitors will implement this paradigm as well, in order to stay competitive and successful. This snowball - effect can be visualized within the following figure:

---

[64] see also: [Nest11]: Survey about the relationship between Open Innovation and the Business Development
[65] see also: [Boag11]: Survey about the relationship between Open Innovation and the Business Development

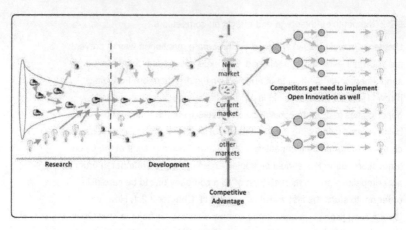

Figure 28: Own Figure, Open Innovation - snowball - effect, cf. [Reic06] , [Ches06]

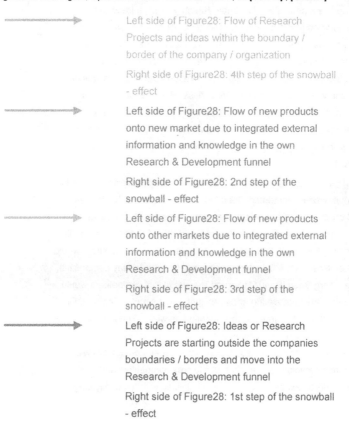

Left side of Figure28: Flow of Research Projects and ideas within the boundary / border of the company / organization

Right side of Figure28: 4th step of the snowball - effect

Left side of Figure28: Flow of new products onto new market due to integrated external information and knowledge in the own Research & Development funnel

Right side of Figure28: 2nd step of the snowball - effect

Left side of Figure28: Flow of new products onto other markets due to integrated external information and knowledge in the own Research & Development funnel

Right side of Figure28: 3rd step of the snowball - effect

Left side of Figure28: Ideas or Research Projects are starting outside the companies boundaries / borders and move into the Research & Development funnel

Right side of Figure28: 1st step of the snowball - effect

Resumé

Within this thesis / dissertation it has been determined how the Open Innovation - paradigm come about. In regards to D. Nobelius [Nobe04] it is a part of the fifth generation of Research & Development management (cf. Chapter 1.1), which considers Research & Development as a network. The differences between the opening up of organizational boundaries and traditional approaches has been determined as well. It was noticeable, that the opening up can lead to technology breakthroughs due to external ideas, knowledge as well as information (cf. Chapter 1.2). Ditto it has been demonstrated, that the opening up doesn't implicate just advantages. Internal information, ideas and knowledge could go astray during the Research & Development process. Thus scientists could leave an organization in order to build up their own start-up to launch new products on new markets (cf. Figure 4, p. 15).

Hence the Business Development department seeks to achieve diversification, these new markets should be reached with products from the own Research & Development in order to gain competitive advantage (cf. Chapter 2). Therefore Open Innovation could be used to crank up the trend of the new product development (cf. Chapter 2.2.2). New products implicate new markets and therefore new customers. The aim is, that external innovation impulses increase the Research & Development productivity. Thus a Research & Development process without outgoing resources would be the aim of an organization. (cf. Figure 23). In regards to McGrath [Mcgr04] and Henry Chesbrough [Ches06], internal product development have to face limits and recommended the implementation of external expertise like external research projects, venture investing, technology in-licensing or technology acquisitions.

In order to support and consolidate the Open Innovation implementation, Web 2.0 technologies for Information Technology services are quiet useful. Open Source communities offer strong knowledge which is disposable. Examples showed, that some IT - companies already used Open Source programs in order to develop their own products (cf. Chapter 1.3.2). Furthermore companies can use Feedback platforms for the communication with their customers. Therefore the customer gives the ideas for new innovations to former products. Technology marketplaces can be used in order to get external information while remaining anonymously. These marketplaces are a kind of the before mentioned technology acquisitions. Customer surveys can be used like Feedback platforms in order to gain customers' opinion and help therefore developing new products to launch them on new markets (cf. Figure 17). However all these Web 2.0 based IT -

services need a process change right up to the service value web (cf. Figure 9), which allows the interaction to resources beyond organizational boundaries. It has been pointed out, that the implementation of Open Innovation helps to gain new customers on new markets. However a not representing survey pointed out, that Web 2.0 - technologies are already in usage in order to enhance the Open Innovation implementation (cf. Chapter 2.4.2).Furthermore it turned out, that the implementation of Open Innovation helps both, enhancing the Business Development in order to get new customers and to gain competitive advantage (cf. Chapter 2.4.3, Chapter 2.4.4). Competitive advantage is therefore based on the launch of new products and processes as well as the collaboration with other organizations and could lead to sustainable growth and market share. Additionally the implementation of Open Innovation enhance the reach of the businesses. However the thesis / dissertation haven't determined, that Open Innovation can be considered as a panacea for consistent company growth.

The dissertation / thesis assayed, if there are snowball - effects due to the implementation of Open Innovation. It transpired, that increasing Research & Development costs could lead to a cul-de-sac. The investment to implement the approach could be to cost intensive and it need the change in the minds of the people. When there are problems in both implementing the approach to organizational processes and problems in implementing the spirit to the employees, a return to traditional approaches may not be helpful in solving these problems or might be too cost intensive (cf. Chapter 3.2.1). A possible way to prevent this snowball - effect would be, to implement Open Innovation additionally not solitary. Another snowball - effect could be, that competitors of an organization could follow their model and implement the Open Innovation - paradigm as well in order to stay competitive and successful on the market. This has been confirmed by the company survey as well (cf. Chapter 2.4.4 , Chapter 3.2.2).

I think, that the implementation of Open Innovation can help organizations in order to develop their new products with the help of information, knowledge or ideas from outside the organizational boundaries. These new products could help to reach new markets or markets of others'. Thus an organization get the ability to reach new customers. In my opinion it can be a good approach to get business growing and to increase competitive advantage. Therefore I would suggest the usage of Web 2.0 - technologies, which can support the implementation of Open Innovation by enhancing the ability to acquire and to use external technologies, information or knowledge. Open Source Communities e.g. should be used to get ideas from the crowd. After costlier filtering processes, occurring geniuses ideas could lead to new research projects and therefore to new products. Nonetheless the implementation of Open Innovation implicates, that the new spirit and the new processes have to be transferred to employees, scientists and the organizational structure, which carriers the risk of lack implementation and failure costs.

Summarizing it is needless to say that Open Innovation could help the Business Development in order to achieve greater power and competitive advantage but it is still not a panacea for continuous corporate growth.

Table of References

[Abas11]   Abas systems GmbH
HABEL Dokumentenmanagement, eBusiness
http://www.abas.system.de
Internet accessed 06.06.2011

[Alla01]   Roy A. Allan
A history of the personal computer: the people and the technology
Allan Publishing 2001

[Ange07]   Dr. George Angemeier
Ansoff Matrix
ProjektMagazin, 2007
Internet Accessed: 11.06.2011

[Anso65]   Igor Ansoff
Checklist for Competitive and Competence Profiles - Corporate Strategy
McGraw-Hill, 1965

[Alca11]   Alcatel-Lucent
Bell Labs
Internet accessed on 16.06.2011
http://www.alcatel-lucent.com

[Alle69]   TJ Allen , WM Cohen
Information flow in research and development laboratories
Administrative Science Quartlerly, 14(1), pp. 12-19, 1969

[Beck09]   Jochen Beck - DasErste
Mondlandung: Technischer Triumf und Mythos um die Lüge
http://www.daserste.de/wwiewissen
Internet accessed 09.06.2011

[Birk11]   J. Birkinshaw, C. Bouquet, J.-L. Barsoux
The 5 Myths of Innovation
MIT Sloan Management Review, Winter 2011, Vol.52 No.2

[Bowo05]	B. Bowonda, J.K. Racherla, N.V Mastakar and S. Krishnan **R&D Spending Patterns of Global Firms** Research Technology Management, Sept/Oct 2005 Vol.48 Nr.5
[Ches03]	Henry Chesbrough **The Era of Open Innovation** MIT Sloan Management Review, 2003
[Ches06]	Henry Chesbrough **Open Innovation - The New Imperative for Creating and Profiting from Technology** Harvard Business School Press, 2006
[Ches11]	Henry Chesbrough **Bringing Open Innovation to Services** MIT Sloan Management Review, Winter 2011, Vol.52 No.2
[Chesb06]	Henry Chesbrough **Open Business Models: How to Thrive in the New Innovation Landscape** Harvard Business School Press, 2006
[Cord11]	European Commission CORDIS **Seventh Framework Programme** Internet accessed on 16.06.2011 http:/cordis.europa.eu/fp7
[Coso03]	George Constable, Bob Somerville **A century of Innovation: Twenty Engineering Achievements That Transformed Our Li** Joseph Henry Press, January 2003
[Dacr06]	Design Against Crime Research Centre **Why Open Innovation** http://www.designagainstcrime.com, Juni 2011

[Druc88]   Peter F. Drucker
                The coming of new organization
                Harvard Business Review, 66, 1988

[Fett06]   T. Fetterhoff & D. Voelkel
                **Managing Open Innovation in
                Biotechnology**
                Research Technology Management,
                40(3): 1, 2006

[Firs11]   Dean Kamem (First) , K. K.
                Kristiansen (LEGO Group)
                First Lego League
                http://www.firstlegoleague.org,
                Internet accessed on the 06th June,
                2011

[Fost11]   Matt Foster
                Web Server Survey
                http://news.netcraft.com
                Internet accessed 06.06.2011

[Frow11]   Clemens Frowein
                **Virtuelle Weiterentwicklung -
                Forschungsprojekt 2011
                Hochschule Heilbronn**
                Internet accessed on 10.06.2011
                http://forschungsprojekt2011.hs-
                heilbronn.de

[Gall08]   Eva Bilhuber Gallo
                **Building Social Capital in a
                Multibusiness Firm: Lessons from
                a Case Study**
                Gabler, 2008

[Gret08]   Andrew Greta
                What is Business Development?
                http://andrewgreta.com
                Internet accessed 11.06.2011

[Hahn07]   Hermann Michael Hahn - Welt Online
                **Wernherr von Braun - Vater aller
                Raketen**
                http://welt.de/wissenschaft
                Internet accessed 09.06.2011

[Hind07]   Brian Hindo
                   **At 3M, A Struggle Between
                   Efficiency And Creativity**
                   Bloomberg Businessweek, Inside
                   Innovation - in depth June 2007
                   Internet Accessed on the 03.06.2011

[Hyve11]   http://www.hyve.de
                   **Customized Innovation - Vom
                   Fuzzy Frontend bis zur
                   Markteinführung**
                   HyveAG , Munich, Germany
                   Internet accessed 07.06.2011

[Itri11]   Industrial Technology Research
                   Institute (ITRI), Taiwan
                   Services of ITRI - Open Innovation
                   Centre
                   Internet accessed on 16.06.2011
                   http://www.itri.org.tw/eng

[Knor03]   Eric Knorr
                   **Fast-Forward 2010 - The Fate of IT:
                   2004 - The Year of Web Services**
                   CIO Magazin, December 2003

[Kotl05]   P. Kotler, V. Wong, J. Saimders & G.
                   Armstrong
                   Principles of Marketing
                   Pearson Education Ltd, 2005

[Lakh00]   Karim Lakhani, Eric von Hippel
                   **How open source software works:
                   "free" user-to-user assistance**
                   MIT Sloan School of Management
                   Working Paper No. 4117, 2000

[Lewi95]   Peter H. Lewis
                   **Digital Equipment Offers Web
                   Browsers Its 'Super Spider'**
                   The New York TImes, 18. Dec 1995

[Matt11]   Frank Mattes
                   **Interview mit Frank Mattes über
                   "Open Innovation"**
                   Internet accessed on 14.06.2011
                   http://forschungsprojekt2011.hs-
                   heilbronn.de

[Mcgr04]	M.E. McGrath
	Next Generation Product Development: How to Increase Productivity, Cut Coss, and Reduce Cycle Times
	Professional Publishing 2004

[Msfc11]	NASA - Marshall Space Flight Center History Office
	Dr. Wernherr von Braun First Center Director
	http://history.msfc.nasa.gov
	Internet accessed 09.06.2011

[Murr10]	David Kord Murray
	Borrowing Brilliance - The Six Steps to Business Innovation by Building on the Ideas of Others.
	Random House Business Books 2010

[Naas97]	National Academy of Science
	Preparing for the 21st century - Technology and the nation's future
	Office of Congressional and Government Affairs, Washington D.C. , 1997

[Nasa69]	Manned Spacecraft Centre
	Apollo 11 Technical Air-to-Ground Voice transcription
	NASA Historical Reference Collection, NASA Headquarters, Washington D.C. , page 375-77, July 1969

[Mort09]	Dr. L. Mortara, J. Napp, I. Slacik, Dr. T Minshall
	How to implement open innovation
	University of Cambridge Institute for Manufacturing, 2009

[Netm11]	http://www.marketshare.hitslink.com
	Search Engine Market Share May 2011
	Internet accessed on the 03.06.2011

[Oecd05]   Meeting of the Organisation for
Economic Co-operation and
Development Council
Growth in Services
OECD Publications, France, 2005

[Pill06]   Frank Piller
**Produktentwicklung mit Hilfe der
Web-Community**
Sap.info: Tägliche Impulse für
Business und IT
http://de.sap.info
Internet accessed 07.06.2011

[Pind09]   R. Pindyck , D. Rubinfeld
Mikroökonomie
Pearson Studium, 2009

[Port85]   M.E. Porter
**Competitive Advantage: Creating
and Sustaining Superior
Performance**
New York Free Press, 1985, p.37

[Quot11]   Quote Database
**Miscellaneous - Quotation Albert
Einstein**
http://www.quotedb.com/quotes/2112
Internet accessed 11.06.2011

[Reic06]   Ralf Reichwald, Frank Piller
**Interaktive Wertschöpfung - Open
Innovation, Individualisierung und
neue Formen der Arbeitsteilung**
Gabler, 2006

[Reic05]   Ralf Reichwald, Frank Piller
**Open Innovation: Kunden als
Partner im Innovationsprozess**

TU - München, 2005

[Ross06]   Shane Ross
**Important Events in Human
History**

CDS CalTech (California Institute of

Technology), January 2006

[Schr09]   Alexander Schroll
                  **First results of the open
                  innovation study**

                  Internet accessed on 09.06.2011

                  http://www.open-innovation.net

[Schu43]   Joseph Schumpeter
                  Capitalism in the Postwar World

                  Postware Economic Problems, 1943

[Sigl10]   Sebastian Sigloch
                  **Eingliederung im Application
                  Management als serviceorientierte
                  Schnittstelle des IT-Management
                  nach der ITIL-Prozessdisziplin
                  SLM.**
                  Wissenschaftliche Aufbereitung der
                  Praxisphase, Hochschule Reutlingen,
                  2010

[Sili09]   Serhan Ili
                  **Open Innovation im Kontext der
                  Integrierten Produktentwicklung
                  Strategien zur Steigerung der FuE
                  - Produktivität**

                  Institut für Produktentwicklung

                  (IPEK), Universität Karlsruhe -

                  Forschungsbericht, Band33, 2009

[Skin09]   Malcolm Skingle
                  **Achieving competitive advantage
                  through Open Innovation**

                  Open Innovation Conference,

                  January 2009, Norwich

                  Internet accessed on 16.06.2011

                  http://norfolknetwork.com

[Thom03]   Stefan Thomke
                  Experimentation matters:
                  unlocking the potential of new
                  technologies for innovation

                  Harvard Business School Press,
                  2003

[Trot05]   Paul Trott
                  Innovation Management and New
                  Product Development

                  Pearson Education Ltd, 2005

[Trot09]   Paul Trott, Dap Hartmann
                  Why 'Open Innovation' is old wine
                  in new bottles
                  International Journal of Innovation
                  Management, Vol. 13, No. 4 ,
                  pp.715-736 (Dec. 2009)

[Tush77]   ML Tushman
                  Technical communication in R&D
                  laboratories: The impact of projekt
                  work characteristics
                  Academy of Management Journal,
                  20, pp624-645, 1977

[Ward10]   Mark Ward
                  40 years of Unix

                  BBC - News

                  Internet accessed on 16.06.201

                  http://news.bbc.co.uk/2/hi/technology

[Whoi11]   http://www.who.is
                  Whois Lookup for the domain
                  'Yahoo.com'

                  Internet accessed on the 03.06.2011

[Zoll05]   Hans-Dieter Zollondz
                  Marketing - Mix - Die sieben P's
                  des Marketings

                  Cornelson - Pocket Business, 2005

Table of illustrations

www.ingramcontent.com/pod-product-compliance
Lightning Source LLC
La Vergne TN
LVHW092350060326
832902LV00008B/925